GW01018559

Dear Lorne

Dear Lorne

P E T E R   H U N T E R

BROWN
DOG
BOOKS

Published under licence by Brown Dog Books and The Self-Publishing Partnership, 7 Green Park Station, Bath BA1 1JB

www.selfpublishingpartnership.co.uk

ISBN printed book: ISBN: 978-1-78545-117-1

Cover design by Kevin Rylands
Internal design by Andrew Easton

Printed and bound by CPI Group (UK) Ltd, Croydon CR0 4YY

Foreword

You couldn't make it up, we fiction writers like to complain. Despite our efforts, real life has all the best stories.

How these letters came to be written reads like a story. A newly-retired detective returns to his boyhood home to convalesce after a thrombosis, and recalls the same leg being broken when he was eleven in a collision with a motorbike. The rider, a nineteen-year-old Canadian soldier, was keen to make amends and became a family friend before his departure for France where, a month later, despatch riding, he was killed by a sniper. More than half a century passes before the detective, with time on his hands, resolves to go to the Calais war cemeteries in search of his old friend.

You couldn't do better if you made it up: the two boys at either end of their teens; one life cut short in a foreign field, the other long-lived close to home; the re-visiting, literal – back to the boyhood home – and figurative.

And, of course, centre stage, that leg.

It's not a story, though: it's true and I can vouch for it, because

Dear Lorne

in the spring of 1996 Peter Hunter limped into a writing workshop that I was leading at Uckfield library. He was making a habit of a daily walk to the library to read the newspapers and periodicals, and there he'd seen a poster advertising three writing workshops. With time on his hands, he'd decided to give it a go.

That first day, I asked the circumspect gentleman and the circle of chatty ladies to write a letter to someone they hadn't seen for a very long time. They might not know if that person was alive or dead, I said, or they might know that he or she was dead, but they could write the letter anyway.

Peter knew Lorne was dead because that's what the family had been told by the officer who had dropped by at the end of 1944 to fetch the camera that had been left behind.

The letters that Peter ended up writing to Lorne, recounting the accident and the good times before his tragic loss, read like a story: the opening with a bang, the arrival of a stranger from a different world into the midst of small town lives; the war, and the worst possible news; a quest, and a kind of laying to rest.

And that motorbike, there at the start and the end.

All of this makes for a deeply affecting story, but doesn't account fully, I feel, for its power, which comes from its telling. Which is a surprise, perhaps, as Peter was writing to someone he knew to have been dead for over half a century, and doing it as an exercise. The result might be expected to be… well, like an exercise. Self-conscious. Contrived.

It's anything but. These letters are spellbinding. What readers want most of any writer is what is hardest for a writer to be: natural on the page. In these measured but heartfelt letters, Peter does it effortlessly. There's a quiet confidence in his voice as he takes us back and forth across time, and a beguiling gentleness of touch on matters of life and death. He sketches his parents' marriage in all its complexity within a wider world on the brink of profound change - and in the midst of it all is a boy about to break with his childhood.

For all this, though, there isn't much of Lorne. We get a good sense of the young man's genuine, easy-going charm, but otherwise he remains unknown and unknowable, just as he was at the time to Peter. Because this isn't fiction. Peter hasn't made him up. He can only tell it as it was, and give us as much of Lorne as he ever knew.

Lorne was only fleetingly in the life of the Hunter family. The story that Peter tells so beautifully isn't Lorne's, however much we might wish that had been possible. This story is Peter's. If we don't learn a lot about Lorne from these letters, we do see something of the young Peter, of what made the man he grew up to be – a man who, with wry humour, a sharp eye and keen ear, is able to bring back to life on the page those who are long gone.

I have had the privilege of re-reading this elegiac series of letters whenever I've wanted during the past twenty years, but have longed for it to have a wider readership. Now, my wish has been granted.

Within these six wonderful letters is history writ small, which is precisely how it comes to those of us so fortunate as to be left to live our lives in peace.

Suzannah Dunn
June 2016

Suzannah Dunn is the critically acclaimed and bestselling author of thirteen books of fiction, including The Sixth Wife and The Confession of Katherine Howard.

Dear Lorne

Dear Lorne

At last I know where to find you. According to the Commonwealth War Graves Commission, you are in the Calais Canadian War Cemetery or the Canadian War Cemetery at Bergen-Op-Zoom.

Excuse the confusion: I know your first name, not your surname, and there are two Lornes on the regimental roll of honour. Until the local military historian identified the cap badge from the photograph, I did not know where to write.

Two hundred and sixty-seven Argyll and Sutherland Highlanders of Canada (Princess Louise's) died in the war, both Lornes killed in action in 1944.

We met the previous year on the bridge over the River Uck, Arthur and me on the way home from school, you motorcycling down the hill. I lay in the road while the signalman left his box, ran his fingers over my shin and mouthed 'greenstick fracture' to the heads bowed over me. You broke a willow twig to explain what had happened to my leg.

The nurse smiled when you brought the Camel cigarette cards and chewing gum collected from the unit, and she wished she had eyelashes like mine. Silly, the things you remember.

Father arrived to take a statement. He was at the end of his police service, marking time until the end of the war. No longer fearful of

Dear Lorne

a German invasion but with his head full of the clatter of machine-guns from battles fought at your age, he was an expert on war. When he knew you better, he told you to get rid of that blasted machine: a despatch rider is a sniper's dream.

First, the delicate question of compensation. Was he hopeful that a carefully construed statement would infer a degree of guilt? Insufficient, perhaps, to make a prima facie case of careless driving. Speed coming down that hill - a contributing factor - afforded room for negotiation. Canadians were an easy touch: compensation for missing chickens, broken fences, careless jeeps, and paternity orders struck before the real business of war intervened.

Did he frighten you with tales of war? He showed you the photograph of the little girl with the Alice in Wonderland hair, button boots and sad eyes. Written on the back in November 1917, "I am quite well. Save this card. I will tell you about its history when I write. The war will soon be over now. So cheer up!" My father had killed her father with a single shot.

You carried me shoulder-high from the hospital, the plaster cast powdering your tunic. Mother brushed it off with a wedding present: "This brush came from Harrods." Arthur reckoned you were a stevedore from Quebec, no wonder you had strong arms. Swung across your neck I caught a new smell, not of queues, and women on buses, and schoolchildren, but the whiff of grizzly bears and lumberjacks.

Somehow the parcels got through at Christmas and food arrived from home. A special cake and biscuits ('crackers', to you), jelly powders, sweets, sugar, a tin of preserved fruit - and grapes, or so I thought, but they were black olives, bitter and disappointing

Dear Lorne

beyond belief.

In the April of the year you were killed, Mother took our photograph behind the police station, the cap badge identifiable through a magnifying glass, identity tags just visible; I hope they were not needed in Calais or Bergen-Op-Zoom. The cat in the photograph, Timoshenko, was named after the Russian General who instituted the system of training and discipline that helped the Red Army see off the Germans. Father liked that, he preached discipline. But you: no belt, no tie, your cap jaunty – just as well Mother cut us off at the legs so your boots cannot be seen. Then you took a photograph of us. Constable 197, tunic buttoned, medal ribbons testimony to past glories, cap set square, and unsmiling: former lance sergeant 2nd Battalion Coldstream Guards, warmonger and purveyor of bad tidings, reporting for duty. Mother wore her grey slacks, no feminist statement but a ploy to hide corned-beef legs from sitting too near our miserable fire.

We fished, you and I, and saw swifts arrive, diving and zooming like Stukas. We went to an ENSA show, the violinist playing 'The Flight of the Bumblebee' and bowing low, Brylcreem catching the lights. "And now, ladies and gentlemen, I would like to sing for you…….." On the way home, you said, "He was a hot fiddler; not so smart with the vocals." And do you remember the mill pond where we saw an officer from your unit fly-fishing? - forbidden to other ranks and locals. We leaned over the railings, watching the casts. The trout have gone, now, the kids fish for pike over submerged supermarket trolleys.

Then you went - overnight, it seemed, without goodbyes. The

Dear Lorne

officer came to collect your camera and told us you were dead. That would have been August or October, depending on which Lorne you are.

When I hear from Canada I will visit. The Commonwealth War Graves Commission has given precise details where to find you both.

Yours
Peter

———◆———

Dear Lorne

Dear Lorne

    I have heard from Canada. You now have a surname, rank, service number and grave – plot 2, row B, grave 9. You died in August with thirteen of the regiment, just over the River Seine at Igoville. You lie in the Canadian Military Cemetery, Calais – leave the motorway at junction 9, turn left to Saint Inglevert, through the village of Lenbringhen and there you are.

I will be over as soon as I can. My last visit to France was with my father, to Metz-en-Couture Communal Cemetery: most of his platoon are there. He died fifty years after them - the dry winter cough persisted through his last summer and by harvest the bales were too heavy for him. His will, written in pencil on a potato order form, was tucked in the map section of the regimental history. The witnesses, cowman and relief milker, wrote their names and addresses with the care of a school exercise. The solicitor said it was a rum do but would stand up if challenged.

In hospital, he peered intently under the bedclothes, searching the gloom above his feet, and ran his fingers over his upper lip: "Look what that Spanish bugger has done!" - the military moustache gone, flattened to stubble as if by a combine harvester. The orderly was a Philippino but Father would have none of it:

"Pity Franco didn't get the little sod." The doctor took me aside: "It's gone through to the liver."

The following day, in and out of delirium, half-finished sentences were lost like thistledown to the wind: "Keep a sharp look-out........critical night........stretcher bearer........ chinky-chinky Chinamen........Dan Rye pinched my rum........" Smiling at the memory, he raised the bedclothes, searching the gloom.

Wally Arnold turned up at the crematorium, representing the Old Comrades Association, bringing a wreath with a cardboard inset of the regiment's badge. "Sorry about the bugler," he said, "Your old chap would have liked the Last Post, but the battalion is in Northern Ireland." You will remember him, he rode the station motorcycle and fancied your machine. He came unstuck for using the side-car to collect his seed potatoes and pea boughs, contravening the Control of Motor Fuel Order 1942, and they took him off motorcycles – his biggest tragedy of the war.

I travelled with Father on a coach with a party of *I remembers* in blazers and regimental ties. I had a spray of poppies in a box from the British Legion to lay on the grave of Father's platoon commander, who died in 1917. Father had written in the margin of page 154, volume 2 of the regimental history, "Lt. LAING, platoon commander, was a good officer, I found him lying on his back, after dark in the moonlight, about two hundred yards from where we dug in."

Up the country road marked on the map – Gouzeaucourt Station 3 miles - the courier said, "This is a specially requested visit. As is our practice, we afford the courtesy of ten minutes to find the grave and pay respects. The rest of you may then de-bus and visit if you wish. Take particular note of the Chinese graves in the top corner. Be back to leave at fifteen fifty."

I laid the spray and sprinkled the ashes round the platoon. No-one saw me from the coach and I kept quiet about it for fear of breaking some regulation or other. I hope he approved.

Cheers for now.
Peter

Dear Lorne

Dear Lorne

The Veterans Association has sent a photograph taken between September '41 and May '43 outside a café in Kingston, Jamaica: nine soldiers, one drinking from a saucer, another pouring beer, four without shirts, and you, half-profile, second from the left between Len Wheeler and George Worth. I am unsure whether I would have picked you out - the words you said and the way you said them are sharper in my mind than your face. Jamaica must have been an idyllic posting. In a curious way, this may be part of the explanation why Father was unbending.

Mother tried to excuse the aloofness which you must have sensed from him. "Nulli Secundus," she said, with a vehemence usually reserved for German bombers. "That's his motto: Second to bloody none." She could have used his trick of using scripture to support a point; she often mocked him that he thanked God that he was not as other men, calling him a Pharisee. He did undervalue others and saw no sin in it.

'Despise' would be harsh; 'judgemental', more like. He knew what was to come, the preparation for battle is a life or death business. Bronzed and cavalier from a congenial posting, you did not know of the battles that woke him at night. We listened from the next bedroom and knew they were secret.

He stood with Arthur and me on the bridge as the regimental pipes and drums beat retreat, cape slung over his shoulder. We watched the swirl of the kilts and the pride of the drum major. "You boys have seen more action than that lot," he said, and I suppose we had.

Before the Dieppe landings, French Canadians occupied the big house. They were not there long. After a fortnight, their interest in Coopers Poultry Farm could be denied no longer and Father cycled up to the estate to investigate. He knew interrogation was a waste of time, soldiers stick together like crap on a blanket. The best he could hope for was that the regimental police would put a stop to it. The provost sergeant, not unreasonably, sought evidence. Father had none. "Look, Mac, ain't there a war on; these things happen." Father came home seething. "Sod the hens; 'War on', 'War on', what's he know about war? Do you know, the sentry on the main gate was sitting in a deckchair chewing that evil gum stuff! Waved me through! I could have been anybody! What a way to run an army. God help us all."

Preposterous to think that anyone would dress up as a constable in order to infiltrate military barracks, but at that time national propaganda warned us to keep a sharp look out for German spies landing by parachute disguised as nuns. After school, we spent hours in a cornfield high on the hill behind the secret house, waiting for them to drop.

During Father's fortnight of night duty, there were two explosions in the orchard at the back of the billets. Despite the provost sergeant's best endeavours, the cause was not established, so the guard was trebled and the deckchair returned to the greenhouse... and the inventory of thunderflashes at the police station reduced by two.

Why did this last son of thirteen children, born to a gamekeeper in the middle of a wood, carry such arrogance? The youngest son, doted on by older sisters, his place secure in a family that was confident in employment and standing in the village, he was spoilt. In a family photograph, he stands centre-frame, aged about ten, dressed in knickerbockers, waistcoat, winged collar, flat cap, his arm nonchalantly bent, hand on hip, unsmiling, flanked by subservient sisters.

Seven years later, he enlisted in the Coldstream Guards. Three brothers before him joined the County Regiment; the fourth was overcome by The Word at the Mission Hall, registered as an objector and went to prison. Father, by now the tallest, was influenced, he said, by a picture of a guardsman in full dress uniform outside Buckingham Palace. It wasn't that, though; he wanted to be elite.

He found a new world at the depot. Fish and chips in town an adventure, and tomatoes - previously unknown - bright and tempting on display. He slept alongside a crook who told the drill sergeant that he was a boundary rider in Mexico and, to prove it, rolled cigarettes one handed, holding the pouch in his teeth. The first night out of barracks he returned and pissed in Father's boots. Father did not speak of the taunts and humiliations but his pencilled comments written forty years later are eloquent testimony to harsh initiation: "The training sergeant had now joined No. 4 platoon from Caterham. He was well-known to most of us. He was the most disliked NCO I ever met. Most of the bullies I met as NCOs were below average intelligence but he was not and I can only presume that he acted as he did to keep himself at Caterham. The sad part was that the officers knew what he was, but turned a blind eye. He was a good instructor but the biggest bully at the depot. Years later, a first class fighting officer told me that when the sergeant came to No 1 Company, all the officers knew what he was and kept an eye on him but were satisfied with his conduct and that he proved to be a good solider. But he didn't stay long enough to prove anything for he was badly wounded at Langemark and went home. And every man alive today who served under him at Caterham has a common opinion of him."

Father wrote of active service with a lighter touch. He revelled in the comradeship of the front line, acquiring stamina and mental toughness and a self-confidence that remained throughout his life.

Yours
Peter

Dear Lorne

Dear Lorne

A letter from a Mrs. Barbara Batchelor has arrived from Cranbrook, British Columbia. She was a war bride from Parkers Place and has never been back. Her late husband served with you in Jamaica and France, and she heard of my interest from the Veterans Association.

She wrote, "Are you one of the brothers whose mother ran the band for the dances?" You know the answer: when the Canadians came, it gave Mother the excuse to revert to form; for too long, she had been stifled by small town rules.

A committed flapper, she had entered the 1920s with an enthusiasm that had unnerved her family. Her hair Eton-cropped, she smoked using a matching shagreen cigarette holder and case. She bought a two-stroke motorcycle which caught fire on Scaynes Hill on the way to play tennis with young men in striped blazers. The little sepia photographs show her laughing, holding racquets like snow shoes. Eventually, with misgivings, she married Father, accepting the disciplines and conformity expected of a policeman's wife. It seemed to me she simmered through our early childhood, taking time to come to the boil. Your regimental march was 'The Campbells Are Coming', which she hummed through the day as if it were an invitation to join the march. She did so with enthusiasm;

we were encouraged to be good hosts to our visitors from the Commonwealth. The time had come for her contribution to the war effort.

She called the band 'Patriotic Hospitality'. Piano, accordion, violin, saxophone and drums. The accordion belonged to the ironmonger's son, who had been repatriated from a prisoner of war camp in Crete. He had lost an arm. The notice in the ironmonger's shop read 'Enforced sale due to enemy action, one Italian piano accordion with manual – three pounds'. He knew her well enough to say, "I can't undo a bra strap, let alone play this thing." Mother sensed this was not the real problem: "You'll soon find someone nice who doesn't wear one." He didn't look too hopeful, and said to me, "Do us a favour, son, do my shoe laces up for me, there's a good chap."

Three pounds was good enough, it seemed unfair to bargain with a man with a stump.

Father was rattled by her enthusiasm. He had fought in the First World War and knew all about soldiers. The billeting of foreign troops in the town had already caused trouble. Now came a new lot, unbloodied and raw, sunburned and confident from a long garrison posting in Jamaica. He raised immediate objection. "Who takes care of the boys when I'm on duty?" This, though, had been anticipated: we would go with her, chaperones to an innocent adventure. He had a difficult case to defend; the implication of duty in the band's name was compelling.

Whilst he was on duty, Mother filled the house with crashing crescendo. The accordion's inset coloured glass pieces - green, red, white and blue - caught the firelight and threw dancing rainbows on the kitchen wall. The straps cut into her shoulders – it was a heavy instrument for a woman – but she padded with dusters. Untutored, in time she mastered the keyboard, and managed to control the bellows and bass stops which had confounded the ironmonger's son.

The violinist and pianist were sisters. The Misses Fletcher had travelled the world together playing the ocean liners; the war had prematurely retired them. Father knew them as dignified spinsters, vastly experienced professionals who were unlikely to be troubled by callow youths from the prairie. The saxophonist was a medical reject and long after the invasions he appeared before the Justices at Brighton to answer an unspeakable charge which confirmed Father's judgement that he was no threat to the ladies of the ensemble. The quintet was completed by the kettle-drummer from the regimental band, not yet out of his teens. Father could read the signs: he would give 'Patriotic Hospitality' six months at most.

Your regiment arrived in the autumn. It was dry; the park an ideal place to practise war. Father watched the manoeuvres, appreciated the military sense in diverting the river, collected up the brown trout blown sky-high by too much explosive, and guessed that the bivouacs, field kitchen trials and signaller activities were preparations for imminent departure. Yes, six months was about right.

They rehearsed in the Odd Fellows Hall. The sheet music came from Woolworths. I can still hear those tunes in my head. 'Bless You for Being an Angel', 'You Made Me Love You', 'Goodnight Sweetheart', 'Mares Eat Oats and Does Eat Oats and Little Lambs

Dear Lorne

Eat Ivy', 'Wrap Yourself In Cotton Wool', and 'Roll Me Over in the Clover and Do It Again'. Do what? I wondered.

The army lorry came twice weekly to pick us up, backing into the police station yard while the other wives pretended not to watch and hoped we would get our comeuppance. The drum kit, already on board, was held steady between the drummer's knees in tartan trews. The saxophonist, a haemophiliac, sat in the front passenger seat because he dare not risk a knock in the back, and waved unnecessarily at the windows of the police houses. The Misses Fletcher, in matching black ankle-length skirts, scrambled aboard unassisted, and Mother, in daring trousers, cocked her leg over the tail-gate like a man. Do you remember the Saturday when you were duty driver? Appreciating that the tail-gate could not be lowered and that the Misses Fletcher were not for hoisting, you apologised for the difficulty, but the little one, the piano player, said, "It's nothing - try taking to lifeboats in evening dress." Their ship had foundered in the Indian Ocean, after dark, in the winter of '36.

Arthur and I were given French chalk to spread on the floors of village halls, sliding across it before the first dance to make sure it worked. We passed the evening chewing endless gum, sticking it under the seats stacked for the evacuees the following day. We couldn't wait for the last waltz. Couples leaned on each other, heads slumped on partners' shoulders as if overcome by exhaustion, and shuffling around, slower and slower. The lights were dimmed, then turned off by some knowing hand. We could only guess at what was happening. Then the lights were back on and the accordion at its loudest, Mother no longer smiling, and we all came to attention

Dear Lorne

facing the Union Flag. *God Save Our Gracious King, Long Live Our Noble King.* The clapping started, and Mother took her bow.

I will write to Mrs Batchelor confirming that we are the Hunter boys; she may have found something about your family which will be interesting, although I do not want to get too involved as most of her letter is about the Beatles – apparently, she has all their records.

Cheers for now,
Peter

Dear Lorne

Dear Lorne

An explanation is due for this one-sided correspondence. I retired early from the police service, gently pushed - a modern phenomenon - back to Uckfield to the little cottage that Father bought at the start of the war as a place to go should anything happen to him. It fell vacant at just the right time. I let my home in East Grinstead to look out instead on the fields of Bird-in-Eye Farm. During the house move, your photograph inscribed 'Lorne, Pete and Tich, April 1944' was shuffled to the top of the biscuit tin. The rest you know: your identity established.

A writer-in-residence visited the local library to hold three workshops in what used to be the Public Hall – I expect you danced there – and six ladies and I attended. 'Readers and writers of all ages are welcome to any or all of the workshops, no previous experience required. Come to one, come to all, whether you are a first timer or old hand.'

I read the first letter to the ladies of the Heathfield Writers Circle and the photograph of the German orphan was passed round; they guessed she was about twelve, born 1905 or thereabouts, over ninety if still alive. They noted her squint eye and polished boots. Probably dead, all very sad.

The writer-in-residence visits prisons, schools and summer camps, a medicine man travelling from place to place, pedalling cures and elixirs. "Write more," she told me. "Develop the family theme."

This is an apology. The writer wanted a piece of fiction, so I invented the cremation and the ashes in France. Father is buried in the graveyard at Buxted Park. The potato order form was unequivocal: "A sum of money shall be set aside to provide a headstone and kerb similar in material and pattern to that of my sisters, Annie and Jane; the stone shall be one foot higher with suitable reference being made upon it to my first wife, Margaret." You will remember her as Maggie. The stone of the right height, material and inscription with space for another name on it has, in fact, no kerb – kerbs are banned so that motor mowers may pass unhindered. Two spinster sisters and the bachelor brother are nearby in a three decker, brother Will and his wife to the right, Annie and Jane ahead, a shambles of Scottish heather before two more sisters and their parents alongside. Grandfather died six months after I was born; grandmother during the war, unaware of the dog fights overhead. Little Ethel had died of diphtheria before Father was born and she is in the old part of the graveyard under a stone flecked with lichen and softened by rain. Her name cannot be read. The famous yew guards them all.

You crouched in the hollow trunk as if hiding from the enemy, looking up into the branches now propped on sawn-off telegraph poles. I told you the bows used at Agincourt were made from it. Did you know about Agincourt? Scientists say the tree was there before

Dear Lorne

Christ and the Agincourt legend is probably untrue. Required to pump the organ by his headmaster who played it, Father slashed his initials deep into the oak over the pumping handle and, seething with injustice, piddled higher and higher against that yew after every Evensong.

Were you ill at ease in the church? Facing the east window, cap in hand, did you say a soldier's prayer before battle?

Arthur and I were sent off to Sunday school and choir, church was our Sunday home, an acceptable crèche, our parents grateful for time on their own. After the accident, the vicar visited his brave little boy and signed the plaster. A rare visitor. Mother offered him a whisky, hoping he would decline - the one bottle that year being saved for Christmas. Emboldened by her generous measure, he enquired whether she would care to join us at St. Saviours. She declined: unfortunately, she suffered from clinical claustrophobia. Onto his second drink, smaller than the first, the Vicar dismissed the churlish suspicion that the bottle had been won at the twice-weekly whistdrive in the cramped little room, blue with smoke, above the Constitutional Club.

Do you remember when you and the sergeant called Red came across us at the river, fishing the pool where the two streams meet to make deep water? You probably saw us from the bridge. To impress, Mother cast with an exaggerated whip of her arm so vigorous that she shot the float and her wedding ring into the middle of the pool. For a second we saw the ring turn before dropping into clear water. Stripping to underpants, you and the sergeant slipped giggling into the waist-high water, searching for sound footing as the churned

Dear Lorne

mud clouded the stream to a khaki blanket. Mission impossible. Mother called for you to give it up. Military underpants weren't designed for swimming. They clung like transparent wash leather. Hands crossed like those of a footballer in a defensive wall, you assessed the bank and realised it could not be climbed without using fingers. She laughed and without demur threw shirts at you for drying off, and I slipped away to find blackberries a month before they were ready for picking.

At tea, Mother did not mention her loss. Moving her signet ring from finger to finger, she twisted it and the band served its purpose. I do not suppose Father ever knew.

Cheers for now
Peter

Dear Lorne

Dear Lorne

Up at dawn. No breeze or birdsong, the horizon behind
the farm building insipid with clouds slow to lighten.
Not a bad day to cross the Channel.

I wait at the corner shop where we bought sweets. Two ounces
of liquorice cuttings or farthing toffee bars. The ration book and
the money puzzled you, the boxes for pencil ticks. Sugar, Bacon,
Cheese, Fats, Eggs (not required – we kept our own hens), Meat and
personal points for Sweets. You examined each coin, checking its
worth, then paid, and said you did not have a sweet tooth.

I tried to get a spray of poppies from the British Legion lady
across the road, who was on 'searchlights' during the war. She was
expecting them any time, she said: they should come this week,
the tables were already laid out in the hall. Instead, I took the palm
cross from behind the kitchen clock; it had been there since Easter
Communion and would have stayed until next year. Our talisman,
folded in my passport.

The paper boys arrive, skidding cycles expertly against the ice-
cream signs. With no time for conversation, they morosely stuff their
bags. The first to arrive turns to the sports page to check on the line
up for the International. He ignores the headline, PEACE PROCESS
SHATTERED. Despite everything, we are still killing each other.

Dear Lorne

My daughter-in-law had offered to drive: it would be nice for the children to come, too. Would it? Fortunately, we could not find a mutually convenient date.

A friend arrives in his new Polish car. He says, as testimony to its efficiency, that it is fitted with German parts and has a decent boot, which is an important feature as he intends to buy cheap Scotch, Australian wine, cigarettes and cartons of Belgian beer from a British supermarket in France.

I seek the grave of a Canadian in a French Cemetery.

We go by 'Le Shuttle', which will allow plenty of time to find you. Under the Channel for the first time; thirty five minutes.

He suggests we take the coast road to Wissant, the scenic route. At the gun emplacements at Cap Blanc-Nez, he points, "It's over there, on a clear day you can see it from here." Dover, shrouded; two ferries pass, gently throbbing, coming and going.

We pass fields you fought across. Open, flat and newly ploughed, an infantryman's nightmare. Clamps of beet wait to be earthed up, tank traps in the making.

We find you in row B between Private B 46656 Marston and Lance Corporal Victor Smith. The service number suggests that you and Marston enlisted together. Killed on the same day. Lieutenant Henderson is nearby – was he the officer we saw fishing just weeks before? Eight of your regiment in the same row.

We are the first visitors of the day; no footprints in the heavy dew. Mushrooms grow in lush grass between the graves, beautiful mushrooms the like of which I have not seen for fifty years - such a prize – and I wonder if it is sacrilege to pick them.

Dear Lorne

There is little colour, nothing much in flower, the perennials and shrubs waiting for spring. Polyanthus, swollen with rain, will bloom against your stone. I am glad the grandchildren did not come, with their exuberance, trampling the mushrooms.

The book in the wall safe identifies Lorne Andrew Marr. No age. No home. No family antecedents. I return to the graves, shoe welts spraying. Most have an inscription chosen by next of kin. Gospel passages are favoured, 'Remembered Always, Our Eldest Son Forever in our Memories.' You have nothing. Why not? Were they so stricken that the right words could not be found? Another Marr in your regiment was killed at another place two months later. Was he one of your kin?

The visitors' book shows that Canadians will return in spring to leave plastic maple leaf flags and poignant messages. Children from nearby villages, touched by history, write the words for TRANQUIL, VERY SAD, THANK YOU. The English, with their eye for conformity, WELL MAINTAINED. VERY IMPRESSIVE.

I leave the palm cross against your stone and write, 'I found an old friend.'

Yours
Peter

Dear Lorne

About the author

Peter Hunter is the son of a village policeman. The family was posted to Uckfield for the duration of the Second World War.

Following army service in Egypt, Peter joined the same force – East Sussex Constabulary - in 1953.

He served as a journeyman detective, dealing with rural crime. In retirement he lives at East Grinstead in a former police house with his wife, a former policewoman, and retired policemen as neighbours.